SCIENCE TO THE RESCUE
ADAPTING TO CLIMATE CHANGE™

ADAPTING TO DROUGHTS

LARRY GERBER

rosen publishing's
rosen central®

NEW YORK

Published in 2013 by The Rosen Publishing Group, Inc.
29 East 21st Street, New York, NY 10010

First Edition

Library of Congress Cataloging-in-Publication Data

Gerber, Larry, 1946–
Adapting to droughts/Larry Gerber.
    p. cm. — (Science to the rescue: adapting to climate change)
Includes bibliographical references and index.
ISBN 978-1-4488-6846-9 (library binding)
1. Droughts. 2. Drought forecasting. 3. Drought relief. 4. Global warming.
5. Climatic changes. I. Title.
QC929.24.G47 2012
363.34'9296—dc23

                                                                    2011045408

Manufactured in the United States of America

CPSIA Compliance Information: Batch #S12YA: For further information, contact Rosen Publishing, New York, New York, at 1-800-237-9932.

On the cover: A parched valley in Namibia, southern Africa.

CONtents

INTROduction

Most of us take a drink of water for granted. All we have to do is turn on a tap or take a bottle of water out of the fridge. But what if things changed and the water supply was suddenly not reliable or drastically reduced? For many people, this is exactly what is happening. In some parts of the world, finding a drink of clean water has become a life-or-death struggle. Millions of human beings have no regular water supply, and thousands—most of them children—die every day.

When an area's usual water supply is stressed or fails in a way that negatively affects people, animals, and plants, that area is said to be experiencing a drought. In recent years, a catastrophic drought has ravaged eastern Africa. The large peninsula known as the Horn of Africa usually has a dry season and a rainy season each year. In 2008, however, the rains began to fail. Within three years, millions of people were on the move, forced by thirst and famine to find relief elsewhere. Farmers and cattle herders fled parched countryside in Somalia and crowded into refugee camps in

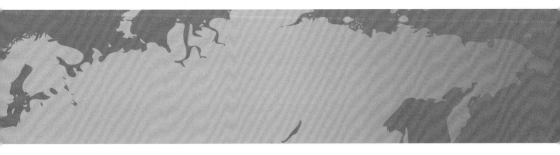

Kenya and Ethiopia. The drought affected eight million to ten million people. Untold numbers died of thirst, starvation, water-borne disease, and other drought-related problems. Drought is hardest on people whose subsistence depends upon their own herds and crops because plants and animals are usually the first to die.

African refugees take water from a polluted stream in Somalia. Waterborne diseases are a major cause of sickness and death during times of drought.

Drought causes problems all over the world. The western parts of North America, as well as huge areas of Asia, Australia, Africa, and parts of southern Europe, are all especially prone to drought. Even places where it usually rains a lot can experience drought. And because droughts threaten food supplies as well as water, they can hurt everybody.

Drought isn't new. It has plagued human communities since the beginning of history. But scientists say human activities—mostly the burning of fossil fuels that release carbon dioxide and other heat-trapping gases into the atmosphere—have caused climate changes that make droughts more likely, more severe, and more frequent.

Is there a solution to the growing specter of drought? One answer seems obvious: generate more water. While the world's freshwater supplies are constantly being recycled in nature, however, the overall amount of freshwater doesn't change. Meanwhile, the world's population is growing rapidly, so more and more people are depending on the availability of and access to that same amount of water.

This looks like a very bleak and daunting picture, but fear and despair don't help much in the search for solutions. Scientists and engineers are working on such solutions: not only finding more water but also making the most of the water that's available. In this book, we'll explore not only cutting-edge research and innovative projects, but also simple, everyday water conservation measures available to all. The problems of global warming and drought are so large that it will require the best efforts of just about everybody living on the planet to solve them.

CHAPTER one

A Delicate System

Earth's water is always moving around the planet and changing its state. Through heating and evaporation, freshwater and salt water change into water vapor that rises into the atmosphere and eventually falls elsewhere as rain, snow, or ice. Falling rain and melting snow eventually find their way back into the ocean and lakes, and the process begins again. This process is called the water cycle.

THE WATER CYCLE

When the sun warms the ocean's surface, water evaporates into the atmosphere, leaving the salt behind. As the water vapor rises, it cools and condenses, forming clouds that bring rain and snow. Some of this precipitation falls on land and seeps underground, forming underground lakes called aquifers. Many communities get their water from wells drilled down into aquifers. Most people on Earth, however, depend on surface water—rivers, lakes, and reservoirs fed by rain, melting snow, or mountain glaciers.

What's causing the drought

Rainfall and snow have been well below normal for almost two years in the Southwest and parts of the East. Some reasons why:

No moisture from tropics

1 High-pressure air system is lingering over central states

2 Pulls high-altitude jet stream north into Canada

3 Jet stream can't pick up moist tropical air that usually brings rain to eastern U.S.

JET STREAM

2

No rain

HIGH 1

What could end the drought

■ Onset of winter and new weather patterns

■ Strong tropical storms in late summer and autumn

Moist air stays in tropics

3

SOURCES: National Weather Service, news reports, MCT Photo Service

This news graphic shows the jet stream, one of the globe's major air currents. The jet stream affects weather over much of North America.

OCEAN CURRENTS AND GLOBAL WARMING

Earth's water cycle is almost too huge to imagine, but it is also very delicate. We tend to think simplistically of the oceans as enormous basins of water. Actually, ocean water is constantly moving. Earth's seas are crisscrossed by currents, which are propelled by differences in water temperature and salinity, or saltiness. Currents move not only across ocean surfaces, but also upward and downward into and out of the depths. These currents are often compared to giant conveyor belts. They carry along warmer or cooler water, which affects air temperature and regulates weather over land as well as over the sea. These currents help determine whether it rains or not in a given region.

The differences in temperature and salinity that drive ocean currents are usually slight. Overall, scientists say, global warming has caused the average ocean temperature to rise about 1 degree Fahrenheit (5/9 of a degree Celsius) over the past one hundred years. That doesn't sound like much, but it has already significantly affected weather in many parts of the world, and the effects will increase as the temperature keeps rising.

Experts trace the recent Horn of Africa drought to an alteration in an ocean current. This shift in the current is known as La Niña. When La Niña is in effect, the ocean current cools surface waters in the central and eastern Pacific Ocean, so that warmer water builds up in the western Pacific. When this happens, Australia and Indonesia get more rain than normal, and west winds strengthen over the Indian Ocean. These winds pull moisture away from east Africa. The result: drought, dead cattle and crops, and millions of thirsty and starving refugees.

Meanwhile, glaciers and ice sheets around the world have been melting faster than ever before recorded, changing the salinity and temperature of ocean currents near the poles.

THE GREENHOUSE EFFECT

Why is the ice melting so fast? Scientists say humans are making Earth hotter by using gasoline, oil, coal, and other fossil fuels that release carbon dioxide into the atmosphere when burned. Carbon dioxide and other "greenhouse gases," such as methane and nitrous oxide, trap heat in the atmosphere, like glass windows trap heat inside a greenhouse. This natural process was first recognized in the 1800s by scientists who called it the "greenhouse effect."

Earth's atmosphere acts like the perfect blanket. It's just thin enough to let the sun's energy get through and warm the planet's surface. Yet it's also just thick enough to shield our planet from the full blast of solar radiation that would burn up all life. It's light enough to allow some of that solar radiation to bounce back into space after it reflects off the planet. Yet it's heavy enough to hold some of the reflected heat in place, so we don't freeze. The greenhouse effect has gotten a lot of bad press in recent years because of global warming, but life on Earth wouldn't be possible without it. The problem today is that we are adding more and more greenhouse gases to the atmosphere, where they are

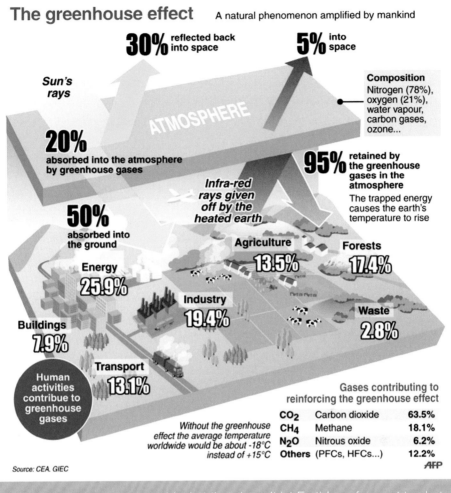

The greenhouse effect
A natural phenomenon amplified by mankind

30% reflected back into space

5% into space

Sun's rays

ATMOSPHERE

Composition
Nitrogen (78%), oxygen (21%), water vapour, carbon gases, ozone...

20% absorbed into the atmosphere by greenhouse gases

95% retained by the greenhouse gases in the atmosphere

The trapped energy causes the earth's temperature to rise

Infra-red rays given off by the heated earth

50% absorbed into the ground

Agriculture **13.5%**

Forests **17.4%**

Energy **25.9%**

Industry **19.4%**

Waste **2.8%**

Buildings **7.9%**

Human activities contribute to greenhouse gases

Transport **13.1%**

Without the greenhouse effect the average temperature worldwide would be about -18°C instead of +15°C

Gases contributing to reinforcing the greenhouse effect

CO₂	Carbon dioxide	63.5%
CH₄	Methane	18.1%
N₂O	Nitrous oxide	6.2%
Others	(PFCs, HFCs...)	12.2%

CO_2 Carbon dioxide 63.5%
CH_4 Methane 18.1%
N_2O Nitrous oxide 6.2%
Others (PFCs, HFCs...) 12.2%

Source: CEA. GIEC

AFP

The atmosphere acts as a blanket that doesn't let Earth's surface get too hot or too cold to sustain life. Human activities—mostly the burning of fossil fuels—are changing the composition of the atmosphere.

accumulating. This has changed the composition of the atmospheric blanket, making it heavier and denser with heat-trapping gases. As a result, the surface and ocean temperatures of Earth are rising.

THE DUST BOWL

From the late 1800s until the 1930s, farmers began turning over the previously unplowed native grasses of the Great Plains to plant wheat and other crops. Life on the windy prairie was often hard, but with adequate rainfall, it was possible to make a living.

In 1931, however, the rains stopped. With the grass gone, there was nothing to hold the dirt in place. Huge wind storms—"black blizzards"—swept up tons of topsoil, making it difficult to breathe and causing lung diseases. As the drought continued, farmers went broke. Thousands packed up and moved away, most heading west to the still fertile valleys of California. This was the largest migration caused by natural disaster in the nation's history. John Steinbeck told the story of fictional "Okie" families—Oklahoma farmers forced to abandon their farms and migrate to California—in his classic 1939 novel *The Grapes of Wrath*.

Sometimes wind carried the dust far up into the atmosphere and far away from the Plains. During the worst storm, in 1934, dust clouds darkened the sky over Washington, D.C., and New York, 2,000 miles (3,219 kilometers) away. Ships 200 miles (322 km) out in the Atlantic Ocean were covered with dust from Kansas.

Through his Soil Conservation Service, President Franklin D. Roosevelt began a program of planting trees and crops, such as legumes and alfalfa. These and other measures helped rebuild the soil and prevent erosion. But the drought continued until 1939, when it finally began to rain again. The so-called Dust Bowl years continue to be the worst drought in U.S. history.

Most climate experts believe these changes are already too extensive and too far advanced to halt or reverse. However, it's hoped that by reducing our output of greenhouse gases, we can slow down global warming before lots of negative cycles are triggered. Once they are triggered, life on Earth will become precarious due to increasing heat, mass extinctions, killer storms, rising ocean levels, severe floods, and catastrophic droughts.

WATER SHORTAGES MEAN FOOD SHORTAGES

An increasing world population makes the problem of global warming–related drought even larger and more complicated. For one thing, it means there is less water to go around. There are twice as many people living on Earth now than there were fifty years ago. However, the amount of the world's freshwater has stayed the same, and most of it isn't available to people.

Most of Earth's water supply is in the oceans and is too salty to drink. Only about 3 percent of Earth's water is fresh. That amount doesn't change much. It is constantly being naturally recycled but not increased. Of the total amount of this already limited supply of freshwater, only a fraction is in places where people and animals can access it. Most of it, about 68 percent, is frozen in glaciers and ice sheets; another 30 percent is underground and out of reach.

A growing population also requires a growing food supply. Increasing the food supply means increasing water usage. It

Drought withers crops and can lead to food shortages and higher food prices.

takes a lot of water to raise animals, grow crops, and process food. Increased farming strains water supplies because many important food crops need irrigation, and cattle and other livestock need water. When water becomes scarce, crops and livestock die. That means there is less food to go around, and the remaining food costs more. Meanwhile, farmers have been burning many of the world's remaining forests to clear land for the crops and animals necessary to increase the food supply for a hungry planet. Yet the process of deforestation sends smoke into the atmosphere and speeds global warming by destroying carbon-absorbing trees. The carbon dioxide that trees would have absorbed is instead emitted into the atmosphere, where it will trap even more heat.

Droughts are equal opportunity catastrophes. They strike wealthy and industrialized countries as well as poor and developing ones. Texas and other southern Plains states, in addition to Florida, suffered severe drought and water shortages in recent years. In 2010, one-third of the huge Russian wheat harvest was lost to drought, further driving up global food prices. Meanwhile, the major farming regions of China, the world's largest wheat producer, were suffering their worst drought in sixty years. The Murray River Basin, in southeastern Australia, was recently ravaged by the country's worst drought in a hundred years. It turned Australia's lush "food bowl" into a dried-out moonscape.

TENSION AND CONFLICT OVER WATER

When water and food become scarce, the risk of war increases. The U.S. Central Intelligence Agency (CIA) has predicted that by 2015, water shortages will have led to tension or fighting in the Middle East, parts of Africa, South Asia, and northern China. Some countries in those regions are already in conflict, and quarrels over water only make things worse. Israel and its Arab neighbors, for example, have been at odds for a long time over access to the Jordan River.

India and Pakistan, mistrustful neighbors who have fought four wars against each other, must nevertheless share a dwindling supply of water from shrinking glaciers in the Himalayas. Both countries have booming populations, increasing the demand for a dwindling supply of water. And both countries,

Glaciers in the Himalayan mountains supply water for people in India, Pakistan, and other countries in southern Asia. As the glaciers shrink, so do water supplies, increasing the likelihood of conflict over the remaining water.

tense and wary of each other, have nuclear weapons. This is a highly volatile situation, one that could ignite if water shortages become acute. Migrations of thirsty refugees and scarce water supplies have also led to arguments among several countries in Africa. The Horn of Africa drought is only the latest example of this.

By 2030, nearly half of the world's population will be living in areas where water is scarce, according to the Organization for Economic Cooperation and Development. Many experts worry that future wars will be fought over water—much as they have been fought over oil and other precious natural resources in the past—as politicians, big corporations, and thirsty people compete for a share of the shrinking global supply.

CHAPTER two

Capturing Every Last Drop

Nobody has ever come up with a way to prevent droughts. However, we can take steps to prepare for them, cope with them, and attempt to minimize their worst effects. Experts sometimes talk about two basic approaches to drought: mitigation and adaptation. Mitigation means making something less serious or less painful. The most obvious way to mitigate drought is to supply more water—to find new freshwater sources or to find new ways to get more water from old sources. Adapting to drought means finding ways to live and work with limited and decreased supplies of water.

DIVERTING SURFACE WATER

Throughout human history, drought mitigation efforts have worked pretty well. People either found new water sources of freshwater or figured out how to move water over considerable distances from existing sources to places where it was most needed. This approach usually involves digging wells or building dams, canals, ditches, aqueducts, and pipelines.

Water projects are as old as civilization. In fact, historians believe that the first civilizations developed in the Middle East when people began to cooperate on the construction and maintenance of the canals and ditches that irrigated their crops. The need for a single leader to coordinate this work may have led to the rise of early kings.

Modern cities and industrial areas could not exist without giant water projects. Southern California is an example. Much of the region is desert. A little over a hundred years ago, officials estimated that the growing city of Los Angeles had enough water to support 250,000 people at most. If people kept moving in, the city would need more water. In 1913, Los Angeles completed an aqueduct bringing water from California's Owens Valley, 250 miles (402 km) to the north. The city later made deals to receive diverted water from the Colorado River and other sources. As more water became available to the city, more people moved there, and demand for still more water continued to grow. The Los Angeles area now imports enough water to support more than ten million residents.

The California Aqueduct carries water from the Sierra Nevada to farms and cities such as Los Angeles. Millions of people depend on huge water projects, but these feats of engineering can create as many problems as they solve.

UNFORESEEN CONSEQUENCES

Massive water-moving projects, while diverting water to where it is most needed, often cause problems that their planners and builders didn't foresee. And even the biggest projects can't meet current demand, so they are often inadequate or obsolete as soon as the construction is finished and they go into service. Central Asia's Aral Sea, once the world's fourth-largest lake, is an example of how water projects can go terribly wrong. In the 1960s, the Soviet Union diverted the rivers that feed the Aral Sea in order to irrigate new cropland. The great lake, which once supported a rich fishing industry, dried up into a polluted sink. The contaminated water caused all sorts of health problems, and the local climate became more severe—colder in winter and hotter in summer. It was one of the world's worst human-made ecological disasters.

The city of Los Angeles also illustrates the conflicts that can arise when water is diverted from one place to another. Farmers in the Owens Valley accused Los Angeles of "stealing" their water, and bitterness remains to this day. Competing demands for water from Southern California's cities, industries, ranchers, and farmers create perpetual friction. The colorful and sometimes violent history of Los Angeles's attempts to secure reliable water sources was the background for the classic 1974 suspense film *Chinatown*.

By the beginning of the twenty-first century, Southern California was using every drop of water that engineers could pipe in from hundreds of miles away. Like many other parts of the world, it had nowhere else to turn for water. Droughts were common in Southern California before anyone had ever heard of global warming. Climate change now makes the area even more vulnerable to drought, water shortages, and conflict over who gets how much.

WATER FROM OCEANS AND CLOUDS

Earth's drinkable freshwater is just a tiny fraction of its total water supply. How can more of it be accessed and delivered to communities? Through the ages, humans have tried to answer this question by diverting and storing freshwater with the help of wells, dams, canals, aqueducts, and pipelines. In the past one hundred years or so, however, people have come up with new ways to tap into the water cycle itself, going directly to the ocean and the sky to test new ways of gathering water. Two of these methods are desalination and cloud seeding.

Desalination is a process by which salt is removed from seawater. Cloud seeding involves the use of airplanes or other means to disperse chemicals—usually silver iodide, dry ice, or salt—into the air. These chemicals can cause cloud condensation or the formation of ice crystals, which can then encourage increased precipitation. In theory, both methods of tapping into new freshwater sources sound great, but each has serious drawbacks.

Desalination occurs naturally as part of the water cycle. When water evaporates from the surface of the ocean, it leaves behind the salt. For a long time, people have known how to mimic this natural process using a method called distillation. If seawater is heated in a container, then allowed to cool and condense, salt and other impurities are removed. One major problem with distillation is that it takes energy of some sort to heat the water. Fuel can be expensive. If fossil fuels are burned to create the heat, the process creates carbon dioxide emissions and other forms of pollution. Another desalination method is osmosis: forcing the water through a thin surface that takes out the salt. However, most methods of osmosis require strong pressure to force the water through, and building up this pressure takes electricity. The energy needed is expensive, and generating it causes pollution.

There are several methods of cloud seeding. Probably the best-known technique is to drop dry ice or silver iodide particles from an airplane into clouds. Without seeding, rainfall occurs when water naturally forms ice crystals near the top of storm clouds. With seeding, the silver iodide or dry ice promotes the formation of ice crystals, making it more likely that rain will fall. This method is called static cloud seeding. Using another method, hygroscopic cloud seeding, gunners on the ground shoot explosive shells full of salts into the lower parts of clouds. The tiny salt particles promote formation of more and bigger raindrops. Like desalination, however, cloud seeding is expensive, and there is disagreement about how well it works.

Dams, canals, pipelines, desalination, and cloud seeding—even when they work well—are simply ways of moving water from one place to another so that people can use it. They divert water. They don't create it. And these diversion methods can no longer keep up with the growth of world population. If we are looking for ways to respond to drought, we have to keep looking for new, more effective, and practical solutions. As Barry Nelson, a senior policy analyst with the Natural Resources Defense Council, told the Associated Press in 2007: "The last century was the century of water engineering. The next century is going to have to be the century of water efficiency."

SMARTER IRRIGATION

Since crop irrigation is one of the main uses of freshwater, many experts are concentrating on finding ways to help

Drip irrigation puts water directly onto plants so that they can get the benefit of every drop. When water is sprayed, plants get only part of the moisture. The rest evaporates.

farmers make every drop count. Farmers struggled with drought long before global warming began, so some of these water-saving methods have been around a long time. They include drip irrigation and underground irrigation. These methods use small pipes and hoses to leak moisture directly onto the roots of crops, rather than spraying from above on the plants themselves. Water that is applied to the roots directly is not wasted, whereas most of the water sprayed from above lands on leaves and evaporates, never making it down into the soil and roots. Another drought mitigation measure is to plant crops that are native to dry climates. These crops tend to be naturally drought-resistant and don't need nearly as much water to thrive.

Recycling is another way to adapt. Irrigation water doesn't have to be as clean as drinking water, so partially treated water from towns and storm runoff can be used on crops. Many states and communities use this "gray" water to irrigate roadside grass and other plants.

CHAPTER three

Tackling the Main Problem

Drought is just one of several problems that are getting worse because of global warming. Many researchers, climate scientists, and organizations, along with some governments and private businesses, are working around the clock and around the world to reduce the negative impact that humans have on the planet's climate.

Most of these efforts are directed at the main cause of climate change—the emitting of carbon dioxide and other greenhouse gases. The great majority of these gases come from the wealthy industrialized countries in North America, Europe, and Asia. The industrialized nations use most of the world's available energy and, as a result, produce the majority of carbon emissions. For this reason, much of the focus in the so-called developed world has been on reducing emissions from factories, cars, planes, and ships.

SEEKING A GLOBAL SOLUTION TO GLOBAL WARMING

The first major international conference on global warming was held in 1979. Participants called on all governments to try to slow down human-influenced climate change. In 1988, the United Nations set up the Intergovernmental Panel on Climate Change (IPCC) and ordered it to study and report on scientific findings from around the world.

What are those findings and where do they come from? People have been studying atmospheric and climate changes in a scientific way for about two hundred years, but reliable weather records for most places go back only one hundred years or so. After World War II, researchers began developing new instruments to record and transmit data on temperatures, atmospheric gases, winds, ocean currents, and other measurements, and began placing these instruments all over the world—in the sky, land, ice, and oceans. They dug into the ocean floor, studied glaciers, and drilled into ice sheets for traces of past climate change. They developed new research methods such as carbon-14 testing to determine the age of things like ancient pollen and seeds. These provided clues to past variations in global climate.

Gilbert Emerson

Cameras mounted on satellites are just one of the many tools that scientists use to collect information about weather and climate on Earth.

The first computer models using some of this data were created in the 1950s. Scientists knew that global warming had taken place in the past and seemed to be occurring in the present. But they weren't sure how fast it could happen or whether humans could cause it. In the following decades, evidence began mounting that the world's currently changing climate was being caused largely by the burning of fossil fuels. It was also observed that climatic shifts were occurring very rapidly—over the span of only a few decades or even years, rather than centuries or millennia as in the past. In 2006, the National Academy of Sciences reported that Earth's overall temperature had risen to the highest point since the last ice age twelve thousand years ago and that it was continuing to heat up.

HOW SCIENTISTS WORK

An estimated 97 percent of climate scientists agree that human activity over the past two hundred years has caused global warming and climate change. By definition, scientists are skeptics. A skeptic is someone who doesn't accept any conclusion until it has been studied, tested, and criticized. When it's time to make their work public, scientists don't simply send their research results to a Web site or a TV station. They make it available for examination and comment by other experts. This is called the peer review process.

If a scientist's work passes peer review, it is then sent out for publication by one of a handful of scholarly journals. These journals are read all over the world by scientists who are free to pick the work apart for errors (and usually do). Scientists can make mistakes like everyone else, but this exhaustive review process means mistakes are usually caught and corrected, and ultimately knowledge is advanced.

Evidence that people were causing the warming continued to come from geologists, atmospheric researchers, oceanographers, and researchers in other fields.

People in many countries called for strong action, but not much was actually done. At the 1992 Earth Summit in Rio de Janeiro, Brazil, 154 countries signed the U.N. Framework Convention on Climate Change and agreed to take action against global warming. The conference set target goals for each country to reduce its greenhouse gas emissions. These targets were only voluntary, however, and many countries failed to meet the goals. At a follow-up conference in Kyoto, Japan, in 1997, most industrial countries made legally binding agreements to reduce their greenhouse emissions. U.S. president Bill Clinton signed the treaty.

A year later, U.S. oil companies, coal companies, and other major polluters joined in a multimillion-dollar campaign to persuade the public that the treaty was based on shaky science. Under energy industry pressure, Congress failed to ratify the Kyoto agreement, and in 2001, President George W. Bush rejected it outright. He said it was too expensive and that it put an unfair burden on the United States because other big polluters like China and India were not required to reduce their emissions.

Was the agreement truly unfair? The industrial countries of Europe and America have been the main contributors to global warming because they have been burning fossil fuels on a large scale for about two hundred years. So the agreement calls on those countries to make the biggest cuts in greenhouse gas emissions and pay to help poorer countries reduce theirs. European countries generally agree with this concept and are taking aggressive steps to cut their greenhouse gas output. Today, China burns more coal than any other country and is reported to be the world's biggest carbon dioxide polluter, with the United States in second place.

REDUCING CARBON EMISSIONS

How can industrialized countries drastically reduce emissions without sacrificing their quality of life? Factories can reduce their greenhouse gas emissions by putting "scrubbers" on

Factories are a major source of the air pollution that contributes to global warming. These cement plants are near the Yangtze River in China.

their smokestacks or by switching to less-polluting fuels like natural gas. Many governments, such as those in Europe and in California, have drastically cut their greenhouse gas emissions by requiring catalytic converters on cars. Some governments and industries place emissions limits on factories and other big polluters, and fine those who go over the limits. Many governments, particularly in Europe, also have restrictions on pollution from airliners and other forms of transportation.

In some parts of the world, including the United States, emissions-trading markets offer another way to reduce large-scale pollution. Businesses in these plans get "credits" that allow them to release a certain amount of carbon dioxide. Cleaner companies may sell their unused credits to companies that pollute more. Some of these credit markets involve whole countries, which may trade credits with other countries. Since the amount of total credits in such plans is fixed, pollution is supposed to stay at or under the fixed level. By reducing the overall number of credits available, governments can theoretically reduce pollution.

Some American communities have tried to organize a nationwide emissions-trading market, but politicians in Congress and elsewhere have stalled the effort. They claim that cutting pollution is too expensive and that governments have no right to force such solutions on businesses and industries. Many of these same people deny that global warming is even taking place.

COMBATING DROUGHT IN DEVELOPING COUNTRIES

Those who suffer the most from drought are usually those who can least afford it—the subsistence farmers and herders who live in the world's poorest countries. People in these countries raise their own crops and cattle for personal use and consumption, and live close to the land. When their crops and cattle die, they have nothing to eat and nowhere to turn. Often they become refugees, leaving home in search of the nearest sources of food and water. The Horn of Africa drought is only one example. The United States experienced its largest disaster-related mass migration during the drought-stricken Dust Bowl years of the 1930s. These migrations can lead to tension or fighting over increasingly scarce supplies of food and water.

Experts are constantly working on ways to help farmers and cattle herders make it through dry times. They include water-saving tools as well as drought-resistant crops. These tools and methods are designed to work in local conditions, and they vary from place to place.

The key words for most developing countries are "sustainable agriculture"—farming and ranching that can be continued indefinitely without depleting the natural resources that make them possible. Instead of cutting and burning forests for new fields or pastures, for example, farmers are

The drought-resistant moringa is sometimes called the "miracle tree" because it has so many uses. It is one of many species that are cultivated because they can survive without much water.

encouraged to plant trees. Tree leaves lock up the greenhouse gas carbon dioxide that would otherwise go into the atmosphere, and they emit oxygen. Tree roots hold moisture and soil in place, preventing heavy runoff of rainwater and soil erosion. They also provide a windbreak, preventing the blowing away of dry topsoil. Drought-resistant tree varieties, such as the moringa, offer other benefits. Known in India as the "miracle tree," the moringa has leaves and pods that can be eaten by humans and animals. Its seeds purify water, and its oil can be used to make soap. It can also be used for fuel and fertilizer.

Instead of huge dams and reservoirs that can ultimately damage sensitive ecosystems and the environment, communities in Africa and elsewhere are turning to community-based water projects. Often helped by volunteers and relief organizations from North America and Europe, community members are drilling wells and building water delivery systems with tools available in the local area. These projects use simple technology that local people can maintain and repair themselves. This allows them to continue operating and maintaining the system even after the aid workers and outside experts leave.

CHAPTER four

Tomorrow's Solutions?

Engineers, climate scientists, researchers, and inventors are constantly coming up with new ideas for dealing with drought, both in developing countries and in the industrial world. Many of these schemes and tools sound like science fiction, and some are, at present, too expensive to consider. But they could become more practical and cost-efficient in the future, and they could save millions of lives if they work. Meanwhile, some cutting-edge drought-fighting products and ideas are simple and cheap.

IDEAS BOTH SIMPLE AND SUBLIME

One of the most interesting of these is the "water machine," which uses natural humidity in the air to produce a home supply of drinking water. Inventors in the United States and Europe developed the device, which sucks in air and condenses it so that the water vapor in the air turns to liquid. An inventor in Texas has sold his version of a water machine, the "Drought Master," for about $500 each. The machine can reportedly produce 5 to 7 gallons (19 to 26 liters) of drinking water a day. The electricity needed to run the machine costs about 4 cents per gallon (3.8 liters) of water produced. At maximum output, that would only cost about 28 cents a day.

For the drought-plagued east African region of Darfur, one proposed answer to persistent water shortages could be giant water-harvesting residential towers shaped like flat-topped mushrooms. In 2007, scientists at Boston University discovered that the Darfur region sits on top of a giant aquifer, one of the biggest in the world. The water is hard to reach, however. A Polish firm designed the towers to be built of clay bricks that could be made locally. The residential towers would pump water up from the aquifer, treat it, store it, and recycle it. People would live in and around the skyscrapers, which are flared out at the top to provide shade. The towers could hold schools, hospitals, and play areas, as well as places to live.

One of the craziest-sounding ideas might not be as goofy as it first appears. For more than fifty years, people have been talking about attaching cables to icebergs in the Arctic and towing them to thirsty regions. The idea has always been too expensive to even try, but recent computer models have shown that it could theoretically be done. A French engineer envisions putting a "skirt" of high-tech fabric around the bottom of the iceberg to prevent melting and using ocean currents to help the towing ships move it to wherever its water is most desperately needed.

MAKING THE MOST OF EXISTING WATER SUPPLIES

New technologies may soon help solve some of the stubborn problems associated with desalination, which is

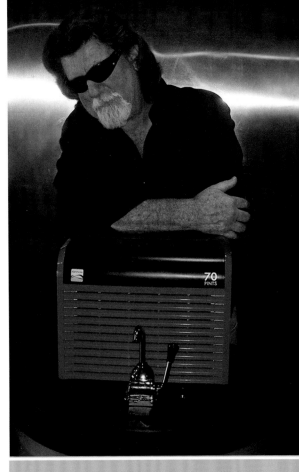

A user poses with an inexpensive water generator. These recent inventions pull moisture from the air and make it available for home use.

extremely expensive and energy-intensive. And, because fossil fuels are used to heat the water and induce evaporation, the process contributes to global warming. However, engineers are combining nanotechnology, the science of manipulating individual atoms and molecules, with a newer method called reverse osmosis to try to eliminate these problems.

Reverse osmosis is one of the most common methods in use today for taking salt out of seawater. In this process,

Barrels can store rainwater that drains from the roof of the house. Harvesting rainwater is one simple and obvious way of adapting to drought and reducing one's "water footprint."

water is forced through a membrane that removes the salt. But the process takes a lot of electricity to generate enough pressure to force the water through. A new type of membrane under development in the United States contains nanoparticles that allow water to pass though more easily, without the need for such high pressure and so much electricity. Another sort of membrane made by Australian scientists uses tiny devices called nanotubes to do much the same thing.

Recycling water is the focus of many drought adaptation plans. New, eco-friendly "smart homes" are equipped to save water and energy in many ways. They capture recycled, or "gray," water that would otherwise go down the drain and use it instead for toilet flushing, lawn watering, and clothes washing. Not all measures have to be high-tech or expensive. People all over the world are making personal "rain harvesting" systems using their own roofs. When it rains, water flows into gutters along the edges of the roof and into storage tanks or rain barrels. The rainwater is then saved and stored in the tanks for later use, often in gardens and on lawns.

Municipal water treatment plants that serve communities can also recycle water. Gray water is safe for all kinds of uses except drinking and bathing. It can be used in place of the fully treated tap water that people normally flush down the toilet or spray on their lawns. Gray water usually comes from earlier stages of treatment at a treatment plant, while drinking water has been fully treated. Less energy is expended when only partially treating water, so using gray water whenever possible reduces one's carbon footprint.

HOW MUCH WATER AM I EATING?

Most of the world's drinking water isn't actually used for drinking—it's used for eating. That is, most of our freshwater goes into food production. It's estimated, for example, that it takes about 625 gallons (2,366 liters) of water to produce a quarter-pound (4 oz; 113 grams) hamburger—and that's just for the meat patty, not the bun or condiments, which require still more water. Why so much?

Most of the hundreds of gallons of water needed to make a hamburger is used to raise feed for cattle (such as corn, hay, or grass). Cows also drink a lot of water. After a cow is slaughtered for beef, more water is needed to clean and process the meat. Then it has to packaged and transported to the market, processes that require more water.

Water is also needed to grow, wash, and transport lettuce, tomatoes, pickles, and wheat for the hamburger bun. If it's a fast-food burger wrapped in paper or plastic, that means even more water went into packaging that's going straight into the garbage can minutes after the customer buys the meal.

In terms of water usage, meat is one of the most wasteful foods we can eat. While it takes 625 gallons (2,366 liters) of water for the quarter-pound beef burger, it takes less than 100 gallons (379 liters) to produce a quarter-pound (4 oz; 113 grams) veggie burger. The amount of water used to grow food and make products is often called the "water footprint" of those things. Just about everything, from potatoes to computers to trucks, has a water footprint. Organizations like Water Footprint Network (http://www.waterfootprint.org) keep track of such statistics.

DROUGHT-RESISTANT CROPS AND SEED PRESERVATION

Drought-resistant crops could save millions of lives. Over the past ten thousand years, throughout the long history of humanity's agricultural efforts, farmers and growers developed many strains of wheat, potatoes, and other food crops specifically adapted to local conditions, including drought. Unfortunately, many of these specialized and perfectly adapted strains are now extinct or nearly so.

As the world's population boomed in the past century and the demand for food grew enormously, farmers all across the planet came to depend on only a few crop varieties that had been developed to produce high yields. Farmers stopped

Heirloom seeds, like these for sale in California, offer the benefit of years of natural adaptation to drought and other adverse weather and climate conditions.

planting the older, local varieties, and they eventually disappeared. An estimated 90 percent of America's historic fruit and vegetable varieties are now gone. Apples are one example. In the 1800s, there were about seven thousand varieties grown in the United States; today, there are less than one hundred. Thousands of varieties of rice were once grown in the Philippines, but today only about one hundred are. The new varieties of crops generally produce more food when planted and grown in ideal conditions, but they aren't tough enough to endure periods of drought or disease.

This ear of corn was genetically engineered by a U.S. company. In laboratories, scientists are developing crops that are genetically modified to be drought-resistant, but these products are banned in some countries.

Botanists and others alarmed by these extinctions have been collecting as many of the older "heirloom" seeds as they can find. Many are stored in seed banks. There are about 1,400 seed banks in the world, including the so-called "doomsday vault" on the Norwegian island of Spitzbergen, 700 miles (1,127 km) from the North Pole. It is built 400 feet (122 meters) above sea level in case the polar ice melts, and its seeds are intended as a backup should the seeds in the world's other banks be destroyed for any reason. Meanwhile, botanists are searching all over the world for any other remaining, previously uncollected heirloom seeds, hoping to keep their traits alive and pass them on.

Some crop-improvement efforts are controversial. In the United States and some other countries, scientists use genetic engineering to create varieties of wheat, corn, and other crops that continue to grow even when stressed by drought. Genetic engineers work with DNA, the molecules that carry genetic information from one generation of living organisms to the next. Using various kinds of laboratory techniques, they introduce DNA from an outside source into a plant. By doing so, they hope to make it or its fruit grow hardier, taller, sweeter, juicier, bigger, less blemished, or pest- and drought-resistant. Many people object to genetic engineering for religious, scientific, health, safety, or business reasons, and European countries forbid it.

CHAPTER five

Take Action!

As individuals, there's not a lot we can do to increase our own supply of freshwater. We can all take steps to adapt to drought, however, and make the most of the water that's already available. This often means changing the way we think, live, and work.

KNOW YOUR WATER

It helps to know where our local water comes from. Most systems draw from rivers, lakes, and reservoirs. Others have wells that tap into aquifers. Ninety percent of Americans get their home water through public agencies. These agencies may be operated by governments, private companies, or a combination of both. They treat and purify water and operate a network of pipes, tanks, and pumps that carry water to homes and businesses.

Since many communities may depend on the same water sources, these agencies often join to form larger districts in order to save money and labor. In the United States, these operations are regulated by the Environmental Protection Agency (EPA), which enforces minimum standards of water quality and safety. In Canada, standards are enforced by Health Canada. In most places, water quality is also monitored by states, cities, counties, provinces, territories, or tribal governments. About 10 percent of homes in America use private wells, many of them not subject to regulation.

Most officials in charge of supplying water to communities in the United States and Canada plan for shortages as part of their jobs. They monitor weather patterns, rainfall, the water level of reservoirs, and snow pack in the mountains that feed the water system. Most systems in the United States equip homes with water meters to determine how much is used, and they may penalize water wasters by making them pay more. In Canada, where water is traditionally plentiful, most systems don't use meters.

DON'T WASTE IT!

Americans use more water than any other people on Earth— about 150 gallons (568 liters) per person a day, according to the U.N. Human Development Program. That doesn't include the water footprint of food and other products we buy and consume. By comparison, Germans use only about 51 gallons (193 liters) per person per day; people in India about 36 gallons (136 liters); and in China, 23 gallons (87 liters). In the poorest countries, such as Haiti and Ethiopia, people get by on about 3 gallons (11 liters) a day.

The average American family of four uses about 400 gallons (1,514 liters) of water a day at home, according to the EPA. About 30 percent of that is used outdoors, mostly on lawns and plants. Toilets account for 27 percent of home water usage. A leaky toilet, however, can waste 200 gallons (757 liters) a day. Here are some simple water-saving steps recommended by conservation experts:

Lawn grass requires a lot of water, and lawn sprinklers are a wasteful way to keep it green.

- Make sure the dishwasher is full before using it.

- Make sure that the clothes washer is full before turning it on. Most cycles use 50 gallons (189 liters) or more of water.

- Wash fruit and vegetables in a bowl of water

instead of using running water. The wash water can then be used on houseplants.

- Store drinking water in the refrigerator; don't let the tap run until the water turns cold.

- Don't let tap water run while brushing teeth. Faucets use 2 to 3 gallons (8 to 11 liters) a minute.

- Fix leaky faucets or ask someone to fix them; one drop per second wastes up to 3,000 gallons (11,356 liters) a year.

Americans use more water per person than any other people on Earth. Adapting to drought means making sure water isn't wasted at home.

- Flush the toilet only when necessary; don't use it as a trash can to dispose of Kleenex and other non-human waste and bathroom products. Consider refraining from flushing liquid waste until it is time to flush solid waste.

- Put a brick in the toilet tank to reduce the amount of water used per flush, or install a low-flow toilet.

- Set the lawnmower blade so that it cuts only the top third of the grass; short cutting allows the sun to dry up the roots and create a "thirstier" lawn.

- Water lawn and plants in the evening so that water can soak in overnight and not evaporate in sunlight.

- Shower instead of taking a bath. Showers require about half the amount of water that baths do.

- Collect rainwater in barrels or tanks, and use it on plants.

SUPPORT GLOBAL ENVIRONMENTAL ORGANIZATIONS

Since 2010, the United Nations has recognized access to clean water as a basic human right. That doesn't mean everyone has a right to free water. But it does mean that governments should make sure everyone has equal access to affordable, safe drinking water. It also means that people who need water for drinking and washing take priority over other water users such as industries.

The United Nations can't change water laws within individual states and countries, however. In the United States, companies, individuals, and governments are free to own,

Glen Canyon Dam and other dams along the Colorado River generate power and provide water to millions of people. Even so, the supply of water is limited, while the demand for it is constantly increasing.

buy, sell—and dispute—water rights. An agreement struck in 1922, for example, divides the water of the Colorado River among eight Western states. Mexico, at the end of the line where the river flows into the sea, wasn't included in the agreement. California and other Western states have been arguing and suing each other for years over how much water each may take. Meanwhile, the once-mighty Colorado River has been dammed and drained all along its length, and Mexico now receives only a small trickle of heavily polluted water.

Climate change and drought are huge issues, and it takes huge steps to deal with them. Individual actions can help, of course. But since the problems were caused by entire societies, it stands to reason that all of society must seek, find, and put into practice a solution. There are many organizations dedicated to transforming the way society approaches the environment and humanity's impact upon it. They primarily strive to reduce greenhouse emissions, slow global warming, and adapt to the negative effects of both, including drought. In doing so, they use a variety of methods.

Greenpeace confronts environmental offenders on land and at sea to draw attention to harmful activities as they are occurring. The Natural Resources Defense Council fights its biggest battles in courtrooms. The Nature Conservancy raises funds to buy open land so that it can't be paved or bulldozed and its waterways can be protected. The Sierra Club takes a grassroots approach, doing everything from monitoring local water supplies to influencing voters. Other groups concentrate specifically on rivers, oceans, wildlife, wilderness areas, farming, entire continents like Africa, or specific regions or parks, like Yosemite National Park.

FACE REALITY

Representatives of industry are often opponents of environmental groups, and they have far more money and more influence over politicians who craft the nation's environmental laws. Industry representatives put forth climate change

WHEN GREEN ISN'T GREEN

Most of the water consumed by U.S. households is used for drinking and washing. But some families routinely dump up to 70 percent of the water they use directly onto the ground. Of all the crops that people grow, lawn grass is one of the biggest water-guzzlers, and we can't even eat it!

A practice known as xeriscaping is one of the best ways for households to save water. It means replacing turf with flowers, shrubs, and other native plants that don't require nearly as much water as grass. Xeriscaping is catching on, especially in dry Western states, where water agencies are raising the costs of water for people who use a lot of it.

Xeriscaped gardens are usually more colorful than plain green lawns, with a much wider variety of plants. They don't have to be all cactus, even though lots of people like to use plants native to their regions. Using underground or drip irrigation systems, landscapers may replace grass with flowers that bloom at different times of year, so there's always some color, even in winter. Xeriscaped lawns also include bushes, shrubs, and other plants that stay green most of the year. And they don't require all the mowing, edging, fertilizing, and other time-consuming, back-breaking maintenance of a grass yard.

"skeptics" who deny that people are causing global warming. Some even claim that global warming, far from being harmful, is actually beneficial to human life. Very few of these paid "experts" are actual climate scientists. Their statements aren't subject to peer review, and they are free to say just about anything they want, no matter how inaccurate or preposterous. Many of their comments and articles are simply attacks on scientists by non-scientists. They may accuse researchers of drawing false conclusions or presenting flawed data, but they seldom offer conclusions or data of their own. They are often influential enough to hire "studies" and plant fabricated news articles claiming to refute real climate science. Some prominent global warming deniers work directly for, and are paid handsomely by, companies in the fossil fuel industry.

Drought can cause great hardship, even in wealthy countries. In eastern Africa and other poor regions, however, even just a trickle of water can mean the difference between life and death.

Many of the world's richest people and corporations worry about losing power or money if they can't keep doing business as usual. Change is seldom comfortable, and massive changes in the way we think, live, and work are bound to be painful, requiring a shared sacrifice across all levels of society. Many of the world's poorest people have already felt the pain of adapting to climate change and drought, losing their crops, herds, homes, and even families. The main question is not whether global warming is real. It is whether everyone should share in the burdens of dealing with it. When it comes to drought and other effects of climate change, there is no denying reality.

GLOSsary

aqueduct A channel for carrying water, usually built above ground and made of bricks, concrete, or stone.

botanist A scientist who studies plants.

condense To become denser or more concentrated.

distill To purify a liquid by first vaporizing it and then condensing it.

divert To make something change course or turn in a new direction.

emission Something that is produced and sent or released into the open.

evaporate To change from a liquid to vapor through heating.

famine An extreme shortage of food.

genetic engineering Changing the hereditary makeup of an organism by introducing or removing specific genes.

heirloom An old, no longer commonly grown or raised variety of plant, vegetable, fruit, or livestock.

membrane A thin, pliable layer of material that serves as a barrier or enclosure.

microbes Microscopic organisms like bacteria that can cause disease.

molecule A group of bonded atoms that make up the smallest fundamental unit of an element or compound.

osmosis The tendency of liquids to pass through a thin, permeable surface from a less concentrated solution to a more concentrated one.

precipitation Rain, snow, sleet, or hail that reaches the ground.

reservoir A basin for holding and storing water, usually created by damming a river.

strain A variety of plant or animal.

trait A genetically determined characteristic.

FOR MORE INFORmation

Environmental Defence Canada
116 Spadina Avenue, Suite 300
Toronto, ON M5V 2K6
Canada
(416) 323-9521
Web site: http://www.environmentaldefence.ca
This Canadian environmental organization promotes envi-
    ronmental protection.

Environment Canada
Inquiry Centre
351 St. Joseph Boulevard
Place Vincent Massey, 8th Floor
Gatineau, QC K1A 0H3
Canada
(800) 668-6767 (in Canada only) or 819-997-2800
Web site: http://www.ec.gc.ca
Environment Canada's mandate is to preserve and enhance
    the quality of the natural environment, conserve
    Canada's renewable resources, conserve and protect
    water resources, forecast weather and environmental
    change, enforce rules relating to boundary waters, and
    coordinate environmental policies and programs for the
    federal government.

Friends of the Earth
1717 Massachusetts Avenue, Suite 600
Washington, DC 20036
(202) 783-7400
Web site: http://www.foe.org
Friends of the Earth and its network of grassroots groups in
    seventy-seven countries defend the environment and

champion a more healthy and just world. Its current campaigns focus on clean energy and solutions to global warming; protecting people from toxic and new, potentially harmful technologies; and promoting smarter, low-pollution transportation alternatives.

Greenpeace
702 H Street NW
Washington, DC 20001
(202) 462-1177
Web site: http://www.greenpeace.org/usa
This global environmental organization has campaigned on environmental issues since 1971.

National Drought Mitigation Center (NDMC)
University of Nebraska–Lincoln
819 Hardin Hall
3310 Holdrege Street
P.O. Box 830988
Lincoln, NE 68583-0988
(402) 472-6707
Web site: http://drought.unl.edu/DroughtforKids.aspx
The NDMC conducts research and provides information on how people can prepare for drought and manage its risks. Its Web site has an extensive student section with information on climate science, drought mitigation, the water cycle, pollution, and many other topics.

National Oceanic and Atmospheric Administration (NOAA)
1401 Constitution Avenue NW, Room 5128
Washington, DC 20230
(301) 713-1208

Web site: http://www.noaa.gov

NOAA is a U.S. agency that studies the atmosphere and the oceans. Its mission is to understand and predict environmental changes so that we can make the best use of our resources. One of its divisions is the National Weather Service. Its Web site has tools and information on practically all aspects of climate science and lots of student resources.

Nature Conservancy
4245 North Fairfax Drive, Suite 100
Arlington, VA 22203-1606
(703) 841-5300
Web site: http://www.nature.org

This is a conservation organization with ongoing projects around the world aimed at the protection of land and water. It identifies principal threats to marine life, fresh-water ecosystems, forests, and protected areas, then uses a scientific approach to save them.

Pew Center on Global Climate Change
2101 Wilson Boulevard, Suite 550
Arlingon, VA 22201
(703) 516-4146
Web site: http://www.pewclimate.org

The Pew Center on Global Climate Change works to develop solutions to climate change.

Sierra Club
85 Second Street, 2nd Floor
San Francisco, CA 94105
(415) 977-5500

Web site: http://www.sierraclub.org
This is one of America's biggest environmental protection
groups and has programs for volunteers to get involved
in protecting water supplies and other resources. Its
Web site has resources for students and links to local
chapters across the United States.

Union of Concerned Scientists
2 Brattle Square
Cambridge, MA 02238-9105
(617) 547 5552
Web site: http://www.ucsusa.org
The Union of Concerned Scientists works to educate the
public about issues relating to climate change.

U.S. Environmental Protection Agency (EPA)
Ariel Rios Building
1200 Pennsylvania Avenue NW
Washington, DC 20460
(800) 438-2474
Web site: http://www.epa.gov
Founded in 1970, the EPA works to shape U.S. environ-
mental policy.

WEB SITES

Due to the changing nature of Internet links, Rosen
Publishing has developed an online list of Web sites
related to the subject of this book. This site is updated
regularly. Please use this link to access the list:

http://www.rosenlinks.com/sttr/dght

FOR FURTHER READing

Aleshire, Peter. *The Extreme Earth Deserts*. New York, NY: Chelsea House, 2008.

Brezina, Corona. *Disappearing Forests: Deforestation, Desertification, and Drought* (Extreme Environmental Threats). New York, NY: Rosen Publishing, 2009.

Chambers, Catherine. *Drought*. Portsmouth, NY: Heinemann, 2007.

George, Charles, and Linda George. *Climate Change Research*. San Diego, CA: Referencepoint Press, 2010.

Gillard, Arthur. *Climate Change* (Issues That Concern You). San Diego, CA: Greenhaven, 2011.

Kaye, Catherine Berger. *A Kids' Guide to Climate Change and Global Warming: How to Take Action*. Minneapolis, MN: Free Spirit Publishing, 2009.

Kusky, Timothy M. *Climate Change: Shifting Glaciers, Deserts, and Climate Belts*. New York, NY: Facts on File, 2008.

La Bella, Laura. *Not Enough to Drink: Drought, Pollution, and Tainted Water Supplies* (Extreme Environmental Threats). New York, NY: Rosen Publishing, 2009.

Lankford, Ronnie D. *Greenhouse Gases*. San Diego, CA: Greenhaven Press, 2008.

Lerner, Adrienne. *Climate Change* (Global Viewpoints). San Diego, CA: Greenhaven, 2009.

Marrin, Albert. *Years of Dust*. New York, NY: Dutton Juvenile, 2009.

Pearson Education. *Science Explorer: Earth's Water* (Student Edition). Upper Saddle River, NJ: Prentice Hall, 2007.

Petersen, Christine. *Renewing Earth's Waters*. Tarrytown, NY: Marshall Cavendish Benchmark, 2010.

Rafferty, John P. *Conservation and Ecology*. New York, NY: Rosen Publishing, 2011.

Salkey, Andrew. *Drought*. Leeds, UK: Peepal Tree Press, 2011.

Van Der Hook, Sue. *The Dust Bowl*. Edina, MN: ABDO, 2009.

BIBLIOGraphy

Associated Press. "Crisis Feared as U.S. Water Supplies Dry Up." October 27, 2007. Retrieved September 2011 (http://www.msnbc.msn.com/id/21494919/ns/us_news-environment/t/crisis-feared-us-water-supplies-dry).

Charles, Dan. "Grainy Season: Engineering Drought-Resistant Wheat." NPR, October 22, 2010. Retrieved September 2011 (http://www.npr.org/templates/story/story.php?storyId=130734134).

Data 360/UN Development Program. "Average Water Use Per Person Per Day." April 15, 2010. Retrieved August 2011 (http://www.data360.org/dsg.aspx?Data_Set_Group_Id=757&transpose=row).

Economist. "UN Climate Talks Pretty Basic." September 3, 2011. Retrieved September 2011 (http://www.economist.com/node/21528247).

Egan, Timothy. *The Worst Hard Time*. New York, NY: Houghton Mifflin, 2006.

Gore, Al. *Our Choice: A Plan to Solve the Climate Crisis*. Emmaus, PA: Rodale, 2009.

Lewandowski, Stephan. "Climate Skeptic Science: Read with Caution." Australian Broadcasting Corporation, September 5, 2011. Retrieved September 2011 (http://www.abc.net.au/unleashed/2870492.html).

Mily, Cynthia A., ed. *Global Warming Opposing Viewpoints*. Farmington Hills, MI: Greenhaven Press, 2006.

New York Times. "Science and Politics of Climate Change." December 12, 2009. Retrieved August 2011 (http://www.nytimes.com/interactive/2009/12/07/science/20091207_CLIMATE_TIMELINE.html).

Reisner, Marc. *Cadillac Desert: The American West and Its Disappearing Water*. New York, NY: Penguin, 1986.

Rosenblum, Mort, and Doug Williamson. *Squandering Eden: Africa at the Edge*. Orlando, FL: Harcourt Brace Jovanovich, 1987.

Siebert, Charles. "Food Ark." *National Geographic*, July 2011. Retrieved August 2011 (http://ngm. nationalgeographic.com/2011/07/food-ark/siebert-text).

U.S. Environmental Protection Agency. "Indoor Water Use in the United States." July 7, 2011. Retrieved August 2011 (http://www.epa.gov/WaterSense/pubs/ indoor.html).

Ward, Diane Raines. *Water Wars: Drought, Flood, Folly, and the Politics of Thirst*. New York, NY: Riverhead Books, 2002.

INDex

A

adaptation, as approach to drought, 17
aquifers, 8, 36, 44

C

carbon emissions, reducing, 26, 30–31
cloud seeding, 21, 22

D

deforestation, 14–15
desalination, 21–22, 37–39
distillation, 22
drought-resistant crops, 24, 32, 34, 41, 43
Dust Bowl, 12, 32

F

food shortages, water shortages and, 13–15
fossil fuels, burning of, 6, 10, 22, 28, 29, 37

G

genetic engineering, 43
global warming/climate change, 6, 9–13, 14–15, 21, 24, 25, 26–29, 31, 37, 50–52, 53
gray water, 24, 39
greenhouse effect, 10–13
Greenpeace, 50

H

Horn of Africa drought, 4–5, 9, 16, 32
hygroscopic cloud seeding, 22

I

Intergovernmental Panel on Climate Change, 26
irrigation, 14, 18, 23–24, 51

K

Kyoto agreement, 29

L

La Niña, 9–10

M

mitigation, as approach to drought, 17, 18, 24

N

Natural Resources Defense Council, 50
Nature Conservancy, 50
Nelson, Barry, 23

O

ocean currents, global warming and, 9–10
osmosis method of desalination, 22

ABOUT THE AUTHOR

Larry Gerber grew up on the Great Plains. Both his parents were survivors of the Dust Bowl, and he frequently experienced heavy dust storms as a boy in the 1950s. A former Associated Press reporter, he has written extensively about water issues in the western United States. He lives in Los Angeles, California.

PHOTO CREDITS

Cover, back cover, pp. 1, 3, 4–5, 49, interior graphics (globe, map) Shutterstock.com; p. 5 Michael S. Yamashita/National Geographic/Getty Images; p. 8 Simmons KRT/Newscom; p. 11 AFP/Newscom; p. 14 Michael S. Lewis/National Geographic/Getty Images; p. 16 Travel Ink/Gallo Images/Getty Images; p. 19 Sarah Leen/National Geographic/Getty Images; p. 23 James L. Stanfield/National Geographic/Getty Images; p. 27 Gilbert Emerson/National Geographic/Getty Images; p. 30 Tim Graham/Getty Images; p. 33 Daryl Balfour/Gallo Images/Getty Images; p. 37 droughtmasters.net; pp. 38, 41, 42 © AP Images; p. 46 istockphoto/Thinkstock; p. 47 Jupiterimages/Comstock/Thinkstock; p. 52 Mike Goldwater/ Getty Images.

Designer: Nicole Russo; Photo Researcher: Marty Levick